READING ELEPHANT PHONICS BOOKS

Sets 1-5: 24 short vowel stories

B. Marker

Copyright © 2021 by B. Marker from Reading Elephant LLC

All rights reserved. No part of this book may be reproduced in any form or by any electronic or mechanical means, including information storage and retrieval systems, without permission in writing from the publisher, except by reviewers, who may quote brief passages in a review.

Table of Contents

Set 1- short a books

Sam Cat 1
The Cat and the Rat 7
Dan and Pam 16
Tap and Jam 24

Set 2- short i books

Kim 32
Bill and Dan 39
Jim is Ill 47
Jill the Pig 55

Set 3- short o books

Tom 61
Off! 69
Bob the Dog 78
Rob the Fox 85

Set 4- short u books

In the Tub 93
Cub Can Run 101
Gus and Bud 110
Gus and Ann 118

Set 5- short e books

Meg the Hen 125
Mex the Rex 131
Ted the Pet 137
Zev's Mess 143
Red Gum 148
The Red Bug 154
Ken the Pup 161
Get to the Top 168

Sight Words

the	again
to	your
a	some
are	water
said	who
was	what
from	one
they	would
you	come
have	could
there	

Teacher Sound Chart

RadingElephant.com

Short vowels – Sets 1-5

a_ hat   e_ met   i_ lit   o_ hop   u_ cup

Consonant Digraphs – Set 6

sh ship   th math / then   ch chop   _ck back   _tch match   wh when   qu_ quick   _ink think   _ank bank

Blends – Set 7

Long vowels – Sets 8-14

a_e make   e_e Pete   i_e Kite   o_e hope   u_e use / duke
ai rain   ee tree   igh light   oa boat   oo moon / look
ay bay   ea seal   _y my   ow glow   ew new
           y funny

R-sounds – Set 15

er clerk   ar dark   or fork
ir bird
ur turn

Other Vowel Digraphs

ow town   au launch   oi soil
ou pouch   aw lawn   _oy joy

C & g rule

c (e, i, y)   g (e, i, y)
face   gem
city   gist
cycle   gym

Inflectional Endings – Set 16

ing   ed
tipping   missed
timing   saved
             rested

Student Sound Chart

ReadingElephant.com

Short Vowels – Sets 1-5
a_   e_   i_   o_   u_

Consonant Digraphs – Set 6
sh   th   ch   _ck   wh_
         tch   qu

Blends – Set 7

Long Vowels – Sets 8-14
a_e   e_e   i_e   _ng   u_e
ai   ee   igh   _ing   oo
ay   ea   _y   _ang   ew
      _y   _ink
                  _ank

R-sounds – Set 15
er   ar   or

ir

ur

Other Vowel Digraphs
ow   au   oi
ou   aw   _oy

Inflectional Endings – Set 16
ing   ed

c & g rule

c (e, i, y)   g (e, i, y)

Permission is granted to reproduce this page (the Student Sound Chart) and this page only, for classroom use only.

Sam Cat

Set 1 Book 1

Focus Sound: Short a

Reading Elephant Phonics Books Sets 1-5

Sam cat.

Reading Elephant Phonics Books Sets 1-5

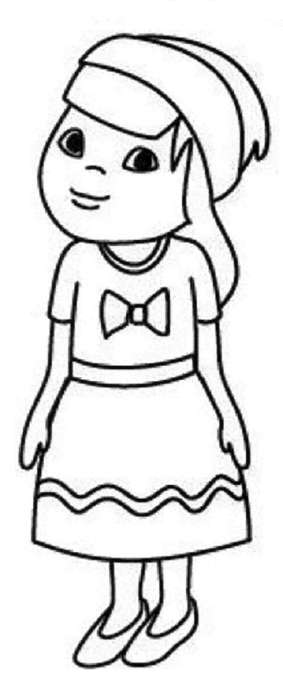

Jan.

Reading Elephant Phonics Books Sets 1-5

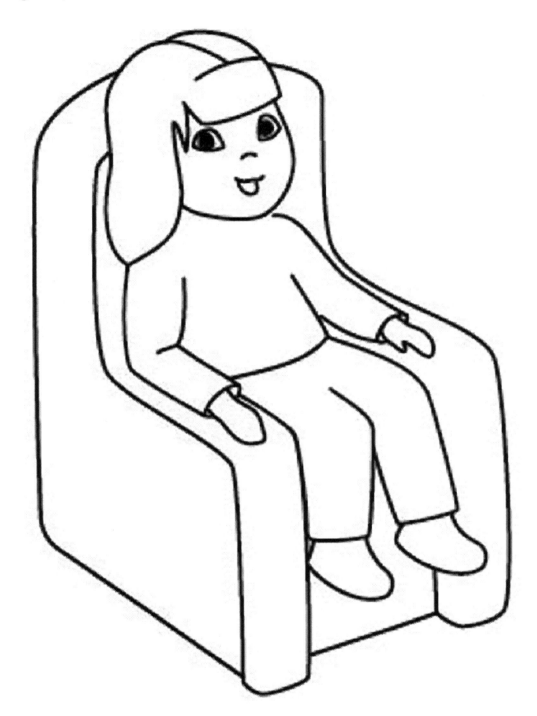

Jan sat.

Reading Elephant Phonics Books Sets 1-5

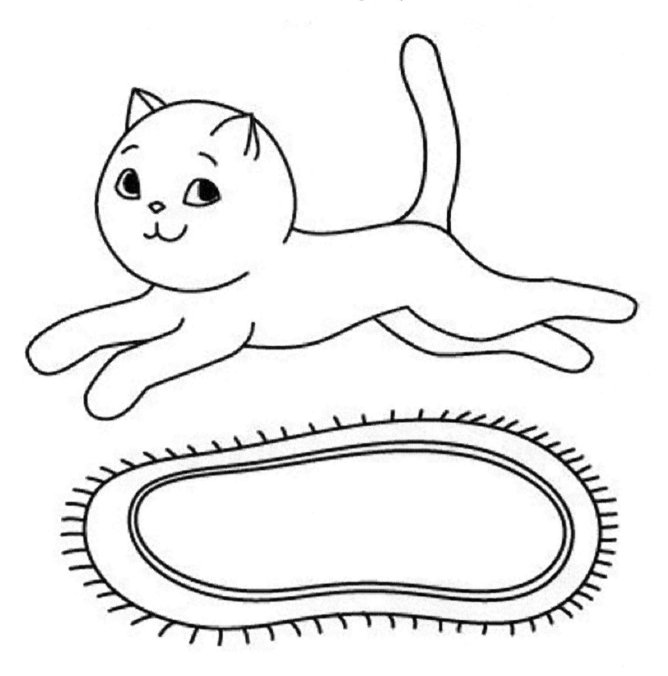

Sam cat ran.

Reading Elephant Phonics Books Sets 1-5

Sam cat sat.

The End.

The Cat and the Rat

Set 1 Book 2

Focus Sound: Short a

Reading Elephant Phonics Books Sets 1-5

Mac rat sat.

Reading Elephant Phonics Books Sets 1-5

Sam cat sat.

Reading Elephant Phonics Books Sets 1-5

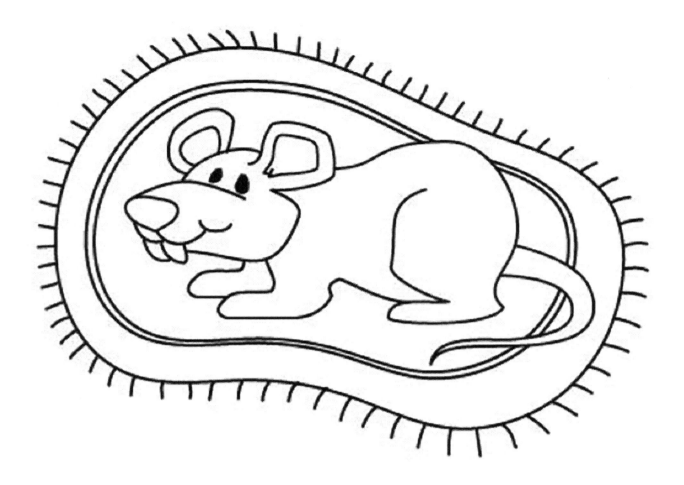

Mac rat ran to the mat.

Reading Elephant Phonics Books Sets 1-5

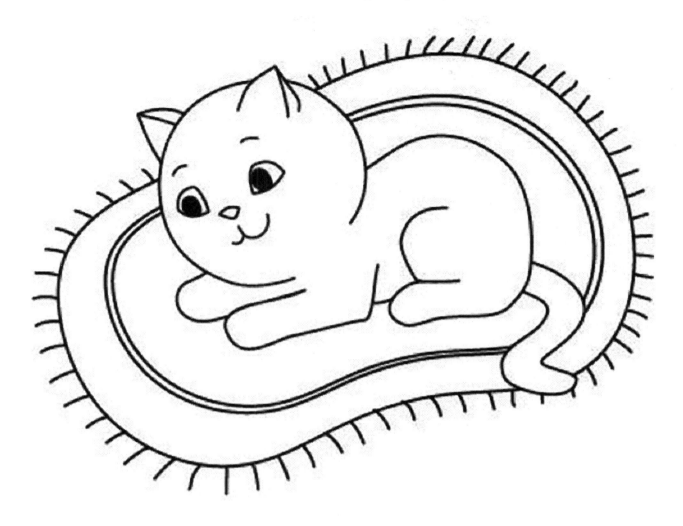

Sam cat ran to the mat.

Reading Elephant Phonics Books Sets 1-5

Mac rat had jam.

12

Sam cat had ham.

Mac rat had a nap.

Reading Elephant Phonics Books Sets 1-5

Sam cat had a nap.
The End.

Dan and Pam

Set 1 Book 3

Focus Sound: Short a

Reading Elephant Phonics Books Sets 1-5

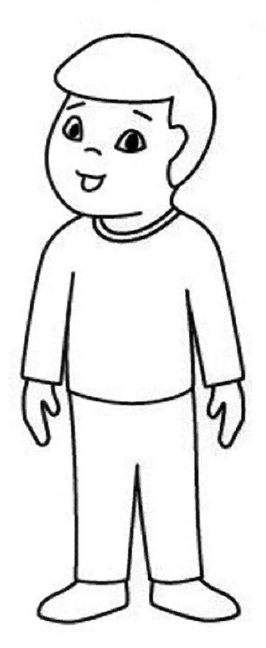

Dan.

Reading Elephant Phonics Books Sets 1-5

Pam.

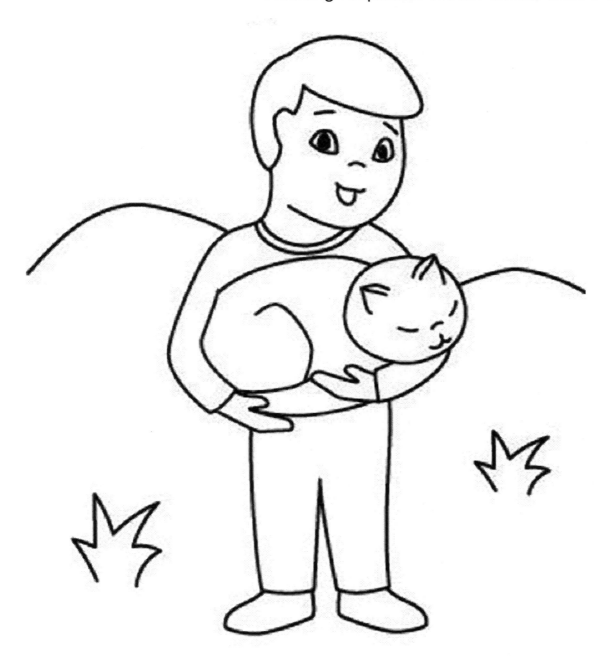

Dan has a cat.

Reading Elephant Phonics Books Sets 1-5

Pam has a bat.

Dan has a rad hat.

Reading Elephant Phonics Books Sets 1-5

Pam has a tan cap.

Dan and Pam are pals.
The End.

Tap and Jam

Set 1 Book 4

Focus Sound: Short a

Reading Elephant Phonics Books Sets 1-5

Pam.

Pam can tap, tap, tap.

Reading Elephant Phonics Books Sets 1-5

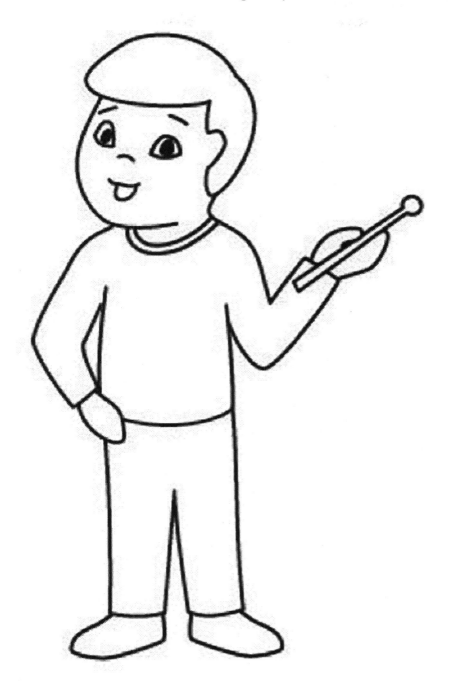

Dan.

Dan can jam, jam, jam.

"Pam can rat-a-tat-tat," said Dan.

Reading Elephant Phonics Books Sets 1-5

Dan has a rad jam.

Reading Elephant Phonics Books Sets 1-5

Sam jams as Pam taps.
The End.

Kim

Set 2 Book 1

Focus Sound: Short i

Reading Elephant Phonics Books Sets 1-5

Kim has a big fin.

Reading Elephant Phonics Books Sets 1-5

Kim is fit.
Kim can swim.

Reading Elephant Phonics Books Sets 1-5

Kim can jig and jam.

Kim can dig, dig, dig.

Reading Elephant Phonics Books Sets 1-5

Kim can tag Tim.

Can Tim tag Kim?
The End.

Bill and Dan

Set 2 Book 2

Focus Sound: Short i

Reading Elephant Phonics Books Sets 1-5

Bill is fit.

Reading Elephant Phonics Books Sets 1-5

Bill ran and ran.

Bill did a jig.

Reading Elephant Phonics Books Sets 1-5

Dan is fit.

Reading Elephant Phonics Books Sets 1-5

Dan can tag Bill.

Bill can tag Dan.

Bill and Dan had a nap.
The End.

Jim is Ill

Set 2 Book 3

Focus Sound: Short i

Reading Elephant Phonics Books Sets 1-5

Jim.

Jim is ill.

Jim has a nap.

Dan is Jim's pal.

Dan will pass it to Jim.

Reading Elephant Phonics Books Sets 1-5

Sip. Sip. Sip

Jim is OK.
The End.

Jill the Pig

Set 2 Book 4

Focus Sound: Short i

Reading Elephant Phonics Books Sets 1-5

Jill the pig.

Jill has six pigs: Mac, Pip, Dan, Kim, Sam and Kip.

Reading Elephant Phonics Books Sets 1-5

Mac, Kim and Sam hid in a big bag.

Kip, Dan and Kim dig in a big pit.

Reading Elephant Phonics Books Sets 1-5

The pigs ran to dad.
The pigs sat on dad.
The End.

Tom

Set 3 Book 1

Focus Sound: Short o

Reading Elephant Phonics Books Sets 1-5

Tom is big.
Tom can hop, hop, hop.
Tom can hop to a mat.
On the mat sat a bag.

Reading Elephant Phonics Books Sets 1-5

Tom has a bag.
The bag is not big.
The bag is not hot.
Tom is mad.

Reading Elephant Phonics Books Sets 1-5

The bag can hop, hop, hop.
It can jig, jig, jig.
It can pop, pop, pop.

The bag is big and hot.
Tom is not mad.

Tom has the big, hot bag.
Tom hops to a log.
Tom sits.

Rip. Tom has a lot.

Reading Elephant Phonics Books Sets 1-5

MMMmmm...
The End.

Off!

Set 3 Book 2

Focus Sound: Short o

Reading Elephant Phonics Books Sets 1-5

Rob the cat was on a mat.
Rob had a nap.
ZZZzzz...

Tim the dog sat on Rob.
Tim did a jig.

Reading Elephant Phonics Books Sets 1-5

Bill the hog sat on Tim.
Bill did a hop.

Rob the cat was mad.
"Off!" said Rob.

Rob got off the mat.
Rob ran.

Reading Elephant Phonics Books Sets 1-5

Bill the hog hit the mat. Bop!

Reading Elephant Phonics Books Sets 1-5

Tim the dog hit Bill. Bop!

Rob sat on Tim and Bill. "Rats!" said Tim. "Off!" said Bill. Rob the cat was not mad.
The End.

Bob the Dog

Set 3 Book 3

Focus Sound: Short o

Bob the dog is a cop.
Bob has a cap,
a map and a rod.

Mac the rat is bad.
Mac hid from Bob.
"I will get Bob's cap," said Mac.

Mac hit Bob.

Mac got Bob's cap.

"Bad rat!" said Bob.

Mac ran. Bob was mad.

Bob ran to the rat.
"Get the cap off!
OFF! OFF! OFF!
The cap is a cop hat," said Bob.

"It is not a rat's hat."
Bob got the cap off Mac.
Mac ran to get a top hat.

Bob has a cop hat.
Mac has a top hat.
Bob the dog is not mad.
The End.

Rob the Fox

Set 3 Book 4

Focus Sound: Short o

Rob is a big fox.
Rob is a dad.

Rob's pups are:
Tim, Jon and Bob.

"I can tag the pups.
The pups can tag dad,"
said Rob.

"Bob can do a jig.
Bob can hop, hop, hop.
Bob can tap, tap, tap,"
said Rob.

"Tim can jog.
Tim is fast. Zip!
Tim can jog and hop,"
said Rob.

"Jon sobs a lot.
Bob and Tim kiss Jon.
They are pals," said Rob.

Jon, Tim and Bob ran to dad.

Rob, Tim, Bob and Jon had a nap.

The End.

In the Tub

Set 4 Book 1

Focus Sound: Short u

Reading Elephant Phonics Books Sets 1-5

Jill is a big pal.
Jill can tag Pam and
Pam can tag Jill.
Uh-oh!
Jill ran in a pit of mud.

Jill did a jig in the mud.
Jill dug in the mud.
"The mud is fun," said Jill.
"But Jill, you have mud on you!
Run to the tub," said Pam.

Jill got in the tub.
"Rub-a-dub-dub.
Jill is in the tub," said Pam.

"There is a lot of mud on the top of Jill," said Pam. "I can not get the mud off. Jill is too big." Jill was sad.

Pam got up on a box.
"I can not rub the mud off the top," said Pam. "Jill is too big."
Jill was mad.

Pam got up on a big box and up on a red box. Pam got the mud off the top of Jill.

"I will not run in the mud again," said Jill.
"I am too big to fit in a tub."
"Yes, you are!" said Pam.
The End.

Cub Can Run

Set 4 Book 2

Focus Sound: Short u

Mom and cub had a nap.
They got up. They sat in the den.
"The sun is up, cub," said mom.
"You can run in the sun,"
said mom. "You can have fun."

"I will get a fig," said the cub.
The cub ran to the fig.
But the fig was up, up, up.
To get the fig, the cub got up
on a box. But the cub was
not as big as his mom.

"I will get the fig cub," said mom.
And the mom got the fig.
The cub bit the fig. "MMmmm...
Thank you mom!" said the cub.

The cub ran to the pond. "Mom!" said the cub. "A fin! I will get it." Zip. The cub ran and ran. "Mom, I can not get it," said the cub. The cub was sad.

"I will get it," said mom.
The mom ran and got it.
"Cub, it is yours," said mom.
The cub bit it. "MMMmmm...
Thank you mom!" said the cub.

Buzz. Buzz. Buzz. "Mom, mom, I will run up, up, up to the bugs," said the cub. The cub ran up. But a big bug bit the cub. "Ug!" said the cub. "I got bit."

"Oh cub! Sit. I will cup some up."
Mom got some. "Have a sip,"
said mom. The cub had some.
"Mmmm.... Thank you mom!"
said the cub.

Mom and cub had fun in the sun. Cub and mom ran to the den to nap. The End.

Gus and Bud

Set 4 Book 3

Focus Sound: Short u

Bud is a pup. Gus is a dad.
Bud can tag dad.
Gus can tag his pup.
They have fun in the sun.

"I can tag you dad," said the pup.
"You can not tag dad," said Gus.
Bud ran to tag his dad.
Gus ran from his pup.
They ran in the water.

Gus got up, up, up. Uh-oh!

The log is big.

"Dad is on the log," said Bud.

"Dad can not get off!" said Bud.

"I will tip the log," said the pup. Tug. Tug.
"I am not big," said the pup.
"I can not tip the log."

"The sun is up," said Gus.
"I am hot. I have to get in the water. I can not sit in the sun," said Gus. The pup got his pal, Bob.

"Dad!" said the pup.
"Bob will tip the log!
The log is not too big for Bob."
Bud and Bob got up, up, up.
Gus got off the log.

"I am off the log!" said Gus.

"Thank you!"

Bud and Bob got a hug from Gus.

They had fun in the water.

The End.

Gus and Ann

Set 4 Book 4

Focus Sound: Short u

Ann was a big cat.
Ann sat in the sun.
It was hot.
Ann had a nap.

Gus got up on Ann.
Hiss. Hiss. Hiss.

Gus bit Ann. "Who bit me?" said Ann. Ann was mad.

Gus got up on Jill.
Ann ran to Jill.
"Off!" said Jill.
"You can not sit on me," said Jill.
Gus ran to a log.

Gus hid in a log.
Ann ran to the log.
Ann did not fit.
"I will hit the log!"
said Ann. Bop!
Ann bit the log too!
Gus ran.

Gus hid in a cup.
Ann ran to the cup.
Ann did not fit in the cup.
"I will sip up Gus,"
said Ann. Sip. Sip.

Ann set Gus on a dog.

Hiss. Hiss. Hiss.

Gus bit the dog.

"Ug!" said the dog. "I was bit.

Who bit me?" Gus ran.

The End.

Meg the Hen

Set 5 Book 1

Focus Sound: Short e

Meg the hen sat on a bed.
Meg got wet. Meg was sad.
"I will not let the egg get wet.
I will sit in the pen," said Meg.

Meg the hen sat in the pen.

Meg had the egg.

It was big and red.

"I will be a mom," said Meg.

Reading Elephant Phonics Books Sets 1-5

Meg set up a bed.
The hen set the egg in the bed.
Meg sat, sat, sat.
Meg had a nap.

The egg did a jig.
The egg did a jam. Pop!
The egg did not have a top.
Meg met Ken.

Meg pet Ken.
Meg fed Ken.
They had fun.
"I am Ken's mom," said Meg.
Meg got a hug and a kiss.
The End.

Mex the Rex

Set 5 Book 2

Focus Sound: Short e

Mex is a big Rex.

Mex was sad.

He did not have a pal.

"I will get a pal," said Rex.

Dan was on a run.

Dan met Mex.

"What a big Rex!" said Dan.

"I will not let the Rex get me."

Dan ran. Mex was sad.

Kel met Mex.

"What a big Rex," said Kel.

"I will not get bit."

Kel hid. Mex was sad.

"I do not have a pal," said Rex, "Not one."

Peg the Rex is big too.

Peg met Mex.

Peg did not run.

Mex was not sad.

Peg and Mex are pals.

Reading Elephant Phonics Books Sets 1-5

Peg has a top hat.
Mex has a red cap.
Peg has a pet rat.
Mex has a pet bat.
They have fun!
The End.

Ted the Pet

Set 5 Book 3

Focus Sound: Short e

"I will get a big, big pet," said Pam. Pam did get a big pet. Pam's pet was Ted.

Pam sat on Ted.

"Run!" said Pam.

Ted ran and ran.

Ted ran in a zig zag.

Ted ran up a hill.

"What fun!" said Pam.

"Ted, sit on the mat.

I will get off," said Pam.

Ted did not sit.

"I do not fit on the mat," said Ted.

Pam was sad.
"I can not get off!"
said Pam. Ted ran and ran.
Ted fell. Pam fell too.

Pam was OK.
Ted was OK.
"I can not sit on Ted,"
said Pam. "I will get Kel.
I can sit on Kel.
What a fun pet!" said Pam.
The End.

Zev's Mess

Set 5 Book 4
Focus Sound: Short e

Zev had a hat, a top, ten pens, a doll and a rag on his bed.
It was a big, big mess.

Zev's mom was mad.

"Get up Zev.

Get rid of the mess!"

Zev was sad.

"Yes, mom," said Zev.

"I will get to the mess."

Reading Elephant Phonics Books Sets 1-5

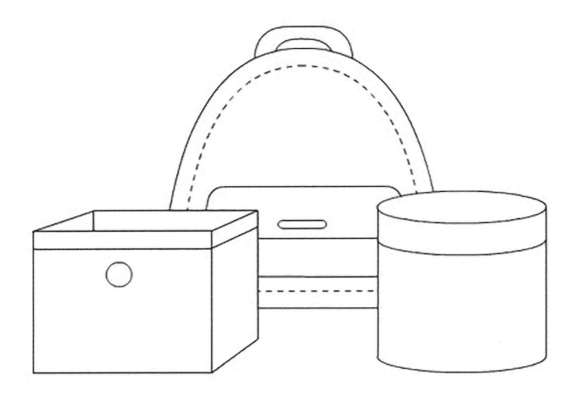

Zev set the hat in a bag.
Zev set the pens in a box.
Zev set the top in a bin.
The doll sat on the bed.

The bed was less of a mess.
Zev's mom was not mad.
Zev was not sad.
"I did it!" said Zev.
The End.

Red Gum

Set 5 Book 5

Focus Sound: Short e

Jan had some gum.
It was red gum.
Jan had a bit.
It got big, big, big.
Jan did not stop.

It got as big as a rat.
It got as big as a cat.
It went up from Jan's lips
as if it were a blimp.
Up, up, up it went.
Will it pop?

Reading Elephant Phonics Books Sets 1-5

POP! The gum was on Jan's lips.
The gum was on Jan's top.
What a mess!

Jan ran to get a rag,
but the gum would not come off.
Jan ran to the tub.

Rub-a-dub-dub

Jan got the gum off in the tub.

The red gum was fun,

but it was not fun to get it off.

The End.

The Red Bug

Set 5 Book 6

Focus Sound: Short e

Jan was a red bug.

Jan sat on a mat.

A big cat sat on the mat too.

"I will get the bug," said the cat.

"What a bad cat!"
said the bug.
The bug ran.
The cat got up.
The cat ran.
The bug went hop
into a big box.

The cat sat in the box.

"What will I do?" said the bug.

The bug was sad.

"The cat is big and
I am little,"
said the bug.
The bug ran to a little spot.
The cat did not fit.

"Cat, come get your ham," said Dan.
The cat ran to his ham.
"Yes!" said the bug.
The bug was glad.

Buzz, buzz, buzz went the bug.
The bug went up, up, up
into the hills.
The End.

Ken the Pup

Set 5 Book 7

Focus Sound: Short e

Ken the pup went in the mud.
What fun!
Ken sat in the mud.
Ken did a jig in the mud.

"What a mess!" said Dan.
"You have to get in the tub," said Dan. Ken did not want to get in the tub. Ken sat, sat, sat.

"You will get some ham if you get in the tub," said Dan. Still, Ken did not get in the tub.

"Ug!" said Dan.

Dan set one hand on his hip.

"Get in pup!

You are a mess!"

Ken did not get in.

"OK," said Dan.

Dan set Ken in the tub.

Plop! Ken was a mad dog.

Dan was wet.

Dan was a mess.

"I have to get in the tub next," said Dan.

The End.

Get to the Top

Set 5 Book 8

Focus Sound: Short e

Mom, Dad and Sis got up to the top. But Sam could not get up.
"I will get up," said Sam.
"I will nip on it too."

Sam got up on a box.
Sam went hop, hop, hop.
He fell off the box and on the mud. Sam was sad.

Sam had a pal, Tom.

Tom could get up, up, up.

"I will sit on Tom," said Sam.

"But you are too big," said Tom. Sam sat on Tom, but Tom could not get up. Sam was sad.

"Dig into it," said sis.
"You can do it Sam!"
Dig, dig, dig went Bob.
He got up, up, up. At the top,
Tom went nip, nip, nip. Yum!
The End.

Made in United States
Orlando, FL
22 January 2023

28939624R00100